Gardening
for
Beginners

Written by Emily Bone and
Abigail Wheatley

Illustrated by Lisa DeJohn

Designed by Helen Lee

Gardening expert:
Hayley Young

CONTENTS

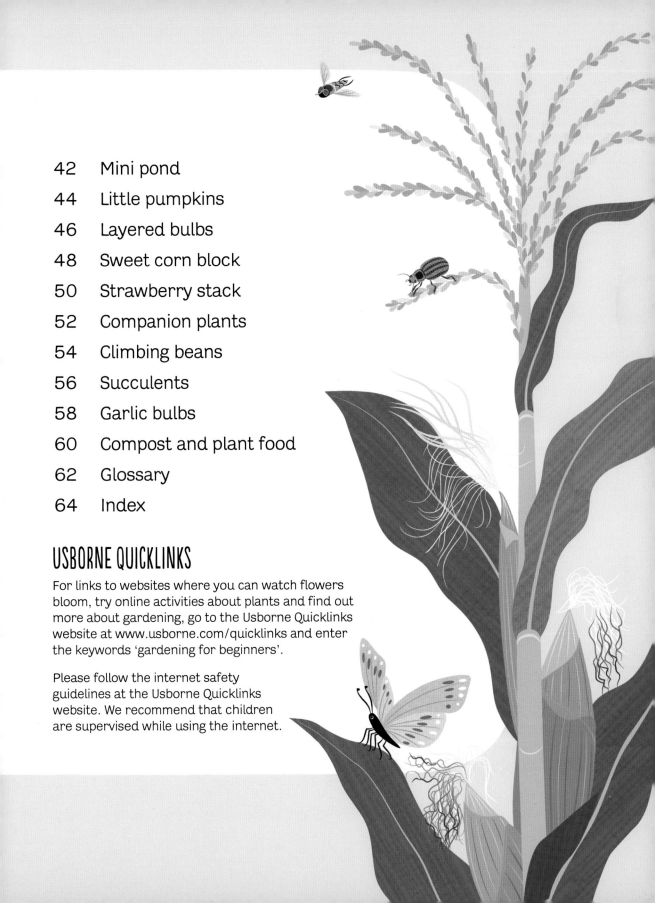

USBORNE QUICKLINKS

For links to websites where you can watch flowers bloom, try online activities about plants and find out more about gardening, go to the Usborne Quicklinks website at www.usborne.com/quicklinks and enter the keywords 'gardening for beginners'.

Please follow the internet safety guidelines at the Usborne Quicklinks website. We recommend that children are supervised while using the internet.

BEFORE YOU START

You don't need a garden to enjoy the projects in this book, as they are all grown in containers. A small outside space such as a balcony or windowsill is fine for many of them. Others can be grown inside.

Before you start a project, read pages 6-15 at the start of the book. Then, read through the project to make sure you have everything you need.

HOW TO USE THIS BOOK

Each project has an introduction to tell you all about it.

There is a list here of everything you will need.

This part tells you where to grow, when to start and and when your plants should be fully grown.

These instructions tell you how to start growing your plants.

There's more growing advice here.

You'll find lots of gardening tips on pages 6-15, and a glossary of gardening words on pages 62-63.

Don't use sprays or chemicals on plants you're going to eat. You can find recipe ideas on the Usborne Quicklinks website, www.usborne-quicklinks.com

Always use the suggested type of plant, compost and container. Use containers with drainage holes, unless the instructions tell you not to. For more about containers, see page 6.

GARDEN SAFETY

What to wear

Wear footwear with covered toes, in case you drop something on your feet. If you're outside and it's sunny, wear sunscreen and a hat.

Animal dirt

If you're gardening outside, watch out for droppings of animals such as dogs and cats. Don't touch them. Ask an adult to remove them.

Soil safety

Getting dirt or compost in cuts can make you ill. Cover cuts or scratches with a plaster before you start gardening. If they're on your hands, wear gardening gloves, too.

If you cut or scrape yourself while gardening, wash the cut straight away and cover it with a plaster.

Take care to avoid getting compost or other dirt in your eyes, too.

For more tips on garden safety, go to the Usborne Quicklinks website, www.usborne-quicklinks.com

Some projects tell you about pests that may attack your plants. You can find out more about pests on pages 14-15.

The things you need to buy for each project are easy to find in garden centres and other shops.

SEED POTATOES

EQUIPMENT

Before you start a growing project, read through the instructions to make sure you have gathered together all the plants, tools and equipment you will need.

A WATERING CAN

When you're watering large plant pots, especially outside, a watering can is useful. It should have a top with small holes (called a 'rose') attached to the spout. This makes the stream of water gentler, so compost, seeds and small plants don't get washed away.

Rose

Large watering cans are heavy when they're full. Use a small watering can, or half-fill a big one.

GARDENING GLOVES

Plant bulbs and some fruit and vegetables such as strawberries and pumpkins can irritate your skin, so wear gardening gloves when handling them. Gloves are also good for protecting your hands from compost, and if you're working with plants that have tough or scratchy stems.

CONTAINERS FOR PLANTS

Each project will tell you what type of container to use. Most plant pots and planters have drainage holes. These allow excess water to escape, to stop the compost from getting waterlogged. If you need to use a container without drainage holes, the project will tell you.

Most hanging baskets don't have drainage holes, but water can still escape.

Drainage holes

Glass jars have no drainage holes.

Drip tray

It's easiest to use bought plant pots, window boxes or other purpose-made planters, as they should come with drainage holes. If you're using them inside, put a drip tray underneath to catch excess water.

CANES & CANE TOPPERS

Some of the plants in this book need to grow up canes. You can buy canes in garden centres. They are often made of wood or bamboo. Buy ones that are the right height for your project, as they can be hard to cut.

You should always put cane toppers on top of your canes. This will stop people from poking or hurting themselves accidentally.

Plastic bottle   Snail shell

You can buy cane toppers, or make your own from small plastic drinks bottles, yogurt pots, small plastic flower pots, or even empty snail shells. Just put a topper upside-down over the top of each cane.

PLANT LABELS

When you're planting seeds, it can help to label them, so you can remember what you've planted in which pot. You can buy plant labels, or make your own from lolly sticks. Write on them in pencil, or using a permanent marker that won't wash off.

Lolly stick

TROWEL

You may find a small trowel helpful for scooping up compost when you're planting things or filling planters with compost.

PENCIL

A pencil is useful for poking small holes in compost, to plant things such as large seeds or cuttings.

COMPOST

Many of the projects in this book use multi-purpose compost. You can buy this from garden centres. Don't use garden soil as it may not be the right type to help your plants grow well.

You can also make your own compost and plant food — see pages 60-61.

PLANT FOOD

Some of the projects in this book suggest you feed your plants with plant food. If you use bought plant food, ask for help and follow the instructions on the packaging very carefully.

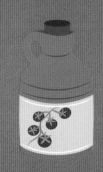

STARTING OFF

Filling pots and sowing seeds in the correct way will give your plants the best possible start and help them to grow well.

FILLING UP

Most projects need a plant pot or planter filled with multi-purpose compost. Here's how to do it:

PLANT POT

1 Scoop compost into the pot you want to fill.

2 Break up any lumps in the compost. If the surface isn't level, press it down gently.

Put a plastic sheet or bag underneath to catch any compost. Then, you can use it again.

PLANTER

1 Use a small pot to scoop compost into the planter. Leave roughly a 1 cm (½in) gap at the top.

2 Break up any lumps in the compost. Then, gently press it down to level out the surface.

Make sure you follow the step-by-step instructions for each growing project, as the tips on these pages might not always be suitable.

ROOTS AND COMPOST

It's essential to have good-quality compost in your pot or planter. Roots suck up food and water from the compost. They also need space to grow.

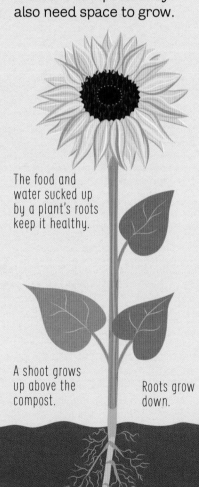

The food and water sucked up by a plant's roots keep it healthy.

A shoot grows up above the compost.

Roots grow down.

SOWING SEEDS

Many growing projects in this book start with seeds. Different seeds need to be sown (planted) in different ways.

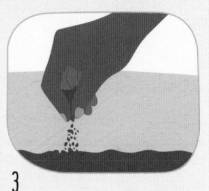

Shoots from small seeds have delicate stems that can only push through a thin layer of compost.

Larger seeds grow thicker, stronger stems, so need a deeper layer of compost around them for support.

SMALL SEEDS

Small seeds are roughly this size:

1 Pour some seeds into your palm. Pinch 5 or 6 between your thumb and first finger.

Make sure you don't scatter too many seeds in one place.

2 Slowly move your hand in a zig-zag line over the compost in your pot or container. Rub your thumb and finger together to drop the seeds.

3 Sprinkle a thin layer (roughly 1cm/½in thick) of compost to cover the seeds. Then, gently press down the compost so it's flat. Water well.

LARGE SEEDS

Large seeds are roughly this size

1 Before sowing, water the compost well, unless the growing instructions tell you not to.

Some seeds need to be pushed in more or less – check the instructions on the seed packet.

2 Take a seed and push it into the compost until it's 3cm (1½in) deep.

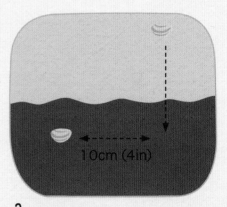

10cm (4in)

3 Push the compost over the hole to cover it, then gently press it down. Make sure you leave at least 10cm (4in) between seeds.

DEALING WITH PLANTS

These pages explain some of the things you might need to do with plants that are already growing.

POTTING ON

'Potting on' is when you move a plant from a smaller plant pot into a bigger planter.

A plant is ready to be potted on if it has a strong stem, three or more fully-grown leaves, and the roots are just starting to grow through the holes at the bottom of the pot, like this.

1

Use the same size plant pot as the plant you're going to pot on.

Keep the scooped-out compost.

Fill the planter with compost. Then, scoop out a plant pot of compost, like this.

2

Gently squeeze and wiggle the pot if it doesn't come away easily.

Put your fingers either side of the plant stem.

Hold the plant in one hand. Then, turn it over so it's resting on your other hand. Carefully pull away the pot.

3

Place the plant in the hole you made in step 1. Use the scooped-out compost to fill in the gaps around the sides and top. Gently press down.

POT-BOUND

If a plant stays in one pot for too long, it becomes pot-bound. This means that its roots fill the pot, so it can't take on food or water from the compost, and starts to die.

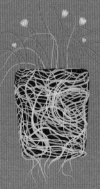

If your plant becomes pot-bound, gently spread out its roots, then pot it on. But, it might not survive.

THINNING OUT

Gardeners often sow more seeds than they need, then cut off the smaller or weaker plants. This is called 'thinning out' and it means that only the strongest and healthiest plants continue to grow. It also gives the growing plants space to develop.

1 When your biggest plants are at least 4cm (2in) tall, look for ones that are smaller, have fewer leaves, or aren't standing as straight as the others.

2 Use scissors to cut these plants off. Check the instructions for each project for how far apart the remaining plants should be – usually 10cm (4in).

If you've sown two bigger seeds in a pair, you could pull out the weaker plant rather than cut it away.

DIVIDING

If two plants are growing well in a small pot, you can pot them both on, rather than thinning them out.

1 Fill two planters with compost, and follow steps 1 and 2 opposite.

2 Carefully ease apart the roots of the two plants, leaving some compost around them.

Try not to break or damage the roots of the plants.

3 Pot on the plants in the planters, as in step 3 opposite.

WATERING AND FEEDING

All plants need water to grow. Too little or too much water will make plants weak, or even die.

Some plants, such as air plants (see pages 32–33), need watering in different ways. Always check the instructions for each project.

WHEN?

Always water before or after you sow seeds, and after you've potted on a plant.

1 Use a watering can to pour water evenly over the surface of the compost. Do this until the compost feels damp.

2 Every other day, poke your finger down into the compost. If it feels moist, the plant has enough water. If it feels dry, add more.

When it's hot and sunny, check the compost every day.

Some plants like more water, and some like less. Always read the growing instructions for each project before watering.

Damp compost will look darker.

Drooping leaves

If your plant's leaves, flowers or stems are drooping, it hasn't enough water. Water the compost around the plant immediately.

Leaf scorch

If water splashes onto the leaves then dries out quickly, it might cause 'leaf scorch', where the leaves turn brown and die.

Water plants in the morning or evening. It's generally warmer during the middle of the day, so any water that's added may dry out before it soaks into the compost.

WHERE?

1 Always water around a plant, not onto its leaves or flowers. Drops of water on a plant might turn mouldy or cause 'leaf scorch'.

2 If the plant is in a drip tray, pour water into that instead of onto the compost. Leave it for an hour.

3 Pour away any water left in the drip tray. The plant has taken in as much water as it needs, and left what it doesn't.

SAVING WATER

Leave a few containers outside. When it rains, these will fill up. Pour the rainwater into your watering can, and use this to water plants. It's actually better for your plants than tap water.

FEEDING

Some plants will grow better if you add extra 'food'. Most plant food is in liquid form, so you can add it to your watering can. Always read the instructions on the packet carefully.

You can also make your own plant food. See page 61 for how.

GARDEN PESTS

Some animals love to eat your plants, and can damage or destroy them completely in a short space of time. Here are some of the most common pests, and tips to help keep them away.

SLUGS AND SNAILS

Slugs and snails love to munch their way through plants with juicy leaves, such as lettuce.

Every time you see a slug or snail on or near your plant, pick it off and put it in an open area of your garden. Then, birds, and other animals that like to eat slugs, will find them.

Snails and slugs need a smooth surface to crawl over. Put down something dry and rough, such as grit, sand or broken up eggshell around your plants. This may deter them from crossing it.

Slugs and snails don't like garlic or strong-smelling herbs, such as chives. Grow these plants next to plants they like to eat.

CATERPILLARS

Caterpillars feed on the leaves and flowers of many plants, especially Asian leaves, nasturtiums and some salad leaves.

Look for holes in the middle or around the edges of leaves and petals.

If you find caterpillars on young plants, pick them off and leave them in a place for birds and other animals to eat them. Older plants shouldn't be too bothered by a caterpillar attack.

It's best to leave some caterpillars in your garden. They turn into butterflies, which are important for pollinating plants.

Caterpillar eggs look like this:

APHIDS AND WHITEFLIES

Aphids and whiteflies are tiny insects that swarm onto the leaves and stems of some plants. They suck out sap – the liquid inside a plant – and keep it from growing properly.

Blackfly

Greenfly

There are lots of different types of aphids. The most common are greenfly and blackfly.

Whitefly

You can help to keep whiteflies away by growing companion plants (see pages 52-53).

Aphids will attack plants, such as climbing beans. But they like nasturtiums more. If you grow a nasturtium near to a bean plant, they might swarm onto the nasturtium instead. Find out how to grow nasturtiums on pages 22-23.

Gently wipe off any aphids you see using a sheet of paper towel.

Fill a clean spray bottle with water. Spray a jet of water onto an area covered in aphids. The jet will blast the aphids off the plant.

Lacewing

Hover fly young

Ladybird

Hover fly

Companion planting (see pages 52-53) can help to encourage bugs that eat aphids and whiteflies, such as ladybirds, and the young of hover flies and lacewings.

FLEA BEETLE

Flea beetles are tiny beetles that chew small, round holes in the leaves of some plants.

Flea beetles attack the leaves of Asian greens, such as this pak choi leaf. They also like to eat potato and radish leaves.

Keep plants well-watered, as the beetles prefer drier conditions. Also, cover young plants with horticultural fleece to stop beetles from landing on them. Older plants should survive an attack.

CATS

Cats won't eat your plants. But they might dig in your compost to use it as a toilet, and uproot plants at the same time.

Orange, lemon or grapefruit peel, or garlic- or onion-smelling plants might help to keep them away.

15

THINGS TO GROW

On the following pages, you'll find
step-by-step instructions on how to grow
all kinds of plants – from a crop of potatoes
in a compost bag, to air plants that don't
need any compost at all.

SUNFLOWERS

Sunflowers get their name from the way they turn to face the sun as it goes across the sky each day. You can grow your own from seeds.

SOW:
MARCH TO MAY

FLOWERS:
JULY TO SEPTEMBER

SITE:
OUTSIDE SUNNY

YOU WILL NEED:

★ 5 seeds from a dwarf sunflower variety such as Choc Chip, Aslan, Teddy Bear or Irish Eyes

★ a plant pot at least 50cm (20in) wide, filled with multi-purpose compost

★ a pencil

1

Use the pencil to poke five holes in the compost, evenly spaced in a ring. Each hole should be around 5cm (2in) deep. Drop a seed into each hole. Sprinkle over a little more compost. Water well.

2

Put the pot in a sunny place outside. Check the compost every few days and water it if it feels dry. In two weeks, you should see tiny green seedlings.

3

Pull out the smaller, weaker seedlings, to leave the three strongest ones in the pot. Keep on watering every few days. In a few more weeks, flower buds should appear.

POTENTIAL PESTS

See the tips on page 58 to keep slugs and snails off your sunflowers. To deter pests such as aphids, try growing chervil or chives nearby as 'companion plants' – see pages 52-53 to find out more.

The flower buds will get bigger and then open into sunflowers.

In the middle of the flower you might be able to see sunflower seeds developing.

When the flowers die, leave them on the plant. As the flowers dry out, the seeds will ripen.

Keep on watering your sunflowers whenever the compost feels dry. Stop when all the flowers have died.

You could collect some seeds and keep them for planting next year. Leave the rest as a snack for garden birds.

SPEEDY VEGETABLES

Vegetable and herb plants can take months to grow. But some can be ready to pick and eat in as little as one week.

Micro-leaves can be picked after their first leaves grow. Spring onions and radishes will go from seed to fully-grown plants in around 4-5 weeks.

MICRO-LEAVES

YOU WILL NEED:

★ a packet of seeds that can be grown for micro-leaves (see below for suggestions)

★ a jar lid

★ paper towel

SOW:
ANY TIME OF YEAR

HARVEST:
1-2 WEEKS AFTER SOWING

SITE:
SUNNY INSIDE

Micro-leaves don't ever grow very big, so they're ideal for a small container, such as a jar lid.

Fennel

Purple basil

Radish

1 Press a sheet of paper towel into the jar lid. Sprinkle water onto it until it feels damp. Then, scatter the seeds over it. Put the lid in a sunny place. Water regularly to keep it damp.

You can grow lots of different vegetable and herb seeds as micro-leaves.

This is kale.

The micro-leaves are ready when the plants have grown their first leaves. Cut away a few plants at a time, just above their roots. They're great as garnishes, or you could put them in sandwiches.

Buy packets of micro-leaf seeds, try the varieties on this page, or any of these:

-Greek cress
-Pea
-Coriander
-Salad rocket
-Beetroot

-Sorrel
-Amaranth
-Fenugreek
-Chard
-Thai basil

FAST GROWERS

YOU WILL NEED:

★ a packet of seeds from a spring onion variety such as White Lisbon or Deep Purple

★ a packet of seeds from a radish variety such as French Breakfast, Cherry Belle, Amethyst or Globe Mix

★ a planter 30cm (12in) wide and at least 15cm (6in) deep, filled with multi-purpose compost, and if growing inside, a drip tray

SOW:
APRIL-SEPTEMBER

HARVEST:
4-5 WEEKS
AFTER SOWING

SITE:
SUNNY INSIDE
OR OUTSIDE

1 Mark a line in the compost halfway across the planter. Water well. Then, sow the different seeds (see page 9).

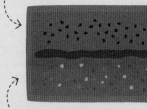

Sow spring onion seeds on this side...

...and radish on this side.

2

When the plants are around 3cm (1½in) tall, cut away the weaker ones so there's at least 2.5cm (1in) between the remaining plants.

Flea beetles, slugs and snails may attack radish leaves and roots. The onion smell of spring onions might help to keep any pests away.

To harvest the plants, gently pull them out of the compost.

Water the plants every other day to make sure the compost doesn't dry out.

Spring onion

Radish

Spring onions will grow thick stems with slightly rounded bottoms.

Radishes grow as small, round roots just under the surface of the compost.

21

NEVER-ENDING NASTURTIUMS

Nasturtiums are bushy plants that grow lots of bright flowers through summer and late into the autumn. The flowers can be eaten in salads and have a slightly peppery taste.

When the flowers die you can collect the seeds to grow more plants next year.

SOW:
MARCH–MAY

FLOWER:
JULY–OCTOBER

SITE:
OUTSIDE SUNNY

YOU WILL NEED:

★ 8 seeds from a nasturtium variety such as Jewel Mix, Empress of India or Alaska

★ a large planter at least 40cm (15in) wide filled with multi-purpose compost

★ a paper towel

★ a clean, dry jar with a lid (for storing saved seeds)

1 Push eight nasturtium seeds into the compost, in pairs. As the plants grow, cut away or pull out the weaker one of each pair to leave four behind. Water them once a week, or more often if the weather is very warm.

2 Flowers will grow, then the petals will droop and fall off, to reveal green balls. These are new nasturtium seeds. When the balls turn to pale brown, take them off and pull apart the seeds.

Each ball is 3 new seeds.

3 Leave the seeds to dry on a paper towel, in a dry, sunny place inside for 2-3 weeks. Store them in a jar in a cool place, such as a fridge, until you're ready to sow them again.

GOOD FLOWERS

Nasturtium flowers are especially attractive to aphids. If you find aphids on other plants, place a pot of nasturtiums nearby. Some of the aphids will move onto your nasturtiums instead. And if the nasturtiums are fully grown, aphids shouldn't damage the plants.

If you don't want to harvest the seeds, cut the flowers when they look like this to use in salads.

Bees love to visit nasturtiums, so plant them to encourage bees.

Don't water nasturtiums too much — they grow better if the compost is slightly dry.

Check around the planter for fallen seed balls.

Some varieties of nasturtium will have trailing stems that spill over the sides of the container. You could sow these in hanging baskets, or grow them up a cane wigwam (see page 54). Check the seed packet to see if your variety is trailing.

BULBS IN A JAR

Some flowers grow from bulbs – bundles formed of fleshy leaves. Bulbs are easy to grow. In the autumn you can buy bulbs that have been treated so they will flower inside in the winter. These are known as 'forced' bulbs.

PLANT:
AUTUMN

FLOWERS:
3-5 MONTHS AFTER PLANTING

SITE:
INSIDE, DARK THEN SUNNY

YOU WILL NEED:

★ around 3 or 4 small flowering bulbs labelled as 'forced' or for indoor flowering, of varieties such as grape hyacinth (Muscari), crocus, dwarf daffodil (also called Narcissus) or dwarf iris

★ a small to medium-sized glass jar

★ some small stones or pebbles, or some gravel

★ multi-purpose compost

★ gardening gloves

1 Arrange a layer of stones or gravel at the bottom of the jar. Add compost, so the jar is half full. Put the bulbs in the middle, with their pointed ends up.

Wear gloves, as bulbs can irritate your skin.

2 Add more compost, so the bulbs are covered, apart from the very tips. Add water until it comes halfway up the stones. Keep the water topped up to this level all the time.

3 Put the jar in a cold, dark place such as a shed, basement or cool cupboard. Check it every week and water it if it feels dry. In 6-10 weeks, you should see pale shoots.

4 When the shoots are 4cm (1½in) high, move the jar to a warm, bright place inside – a windowsill is ideal. Keep checking the compost, and water it if it feels dry.

The shoots will grow taller and flower buds will appear.

Keep on checking the water level and topping it up if you need to, until after the bulbs flower.

When the flowers shrivel, leave the jar for 6 weeks, so the bulbs can store up food for next year. They won't flower inside again, though.

Grape hyacinths

The bulbs are full of stored food that the shoots, leaves and flowers need to grow.

In the autumn, you can plant the bulbs in the ground or in a pot outside. They may flower next year.

Roots reach down from the bulbs to suck up water.

NO COMPOST

You can grow bulbs without compost, but you will also need a piece of charcoal to stop the water from smelling. Barbecue charcoal is ideal.

Half-fill the jar with stones. Push the charcoal in among the stones. Arrange the bulbs on top. Water, so the stones are just covered. Keep the water topped up.

Charcoal

CUT-AND-COME-AGAIN SALAD

You can grow lettuce and all kinds of leafy salad vegetables as 'cut-and-come-again' plants. This means that you cut leaves when you want to eat them, and more will grow in their place.

SOW:
MARCH TO SEPTEMBER

SITE:
AN AREA THAT'S IN SHADE FOR PART OF THE DAY, SO THE PLANTS DON'T GET TOO HOT

HARVEST:
4-6 WEEKS AFTER SOWING

YOU WILL NEED:

★ a packet of lettuce seeds or other leafy salad vegetables (see 'Lovely leaves' opposite)

★ a planter at least 10cm (4in) tall and wide filled with multi-purpose compost. If you're keeping the container inside, you'll need to place it in a drip tray before watering.

Different salad plants have different-shaped leaves, markings and colours. Grow a mix to get a display like this.

Green oak leaf lettuce

Calendula or 'pot marigolds' are edible flowers, a little like nasturtiums (see pages 22-23). They will grow well in between your leaves.

Kale

Beetroot leaves

Slugs and snails might attack your salad leaves, so make sure you protect your plants (see page 14).

Rocket has a spicy taste.

Mizuna

1 Sow around 20 salad seeds by following the instructions on page 9 for how to sow small seeds.

Check the compost every 2-3 days and water if it feels dry.

2 Put the planter inside, or outside, but make sure the area is in shade for part of the day.

Don't throw away the small plants – you can eat them, too.

3 As the plants grow, use scissors to cut away any smaller or weaker ones.

LOVELY LEAVES

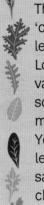

There are lots of 'cut-and-come-again' lettuces to grow. Look for 'loose-leaf' varieties, or try sowing a packet of mixed lettuce seed. You could also grow leafy vegetables as salad, such as kale, chard and beetroot, but don't let the leaves get too big before picking them.

Make sure you keep your lettuce out of direct, very warm sunlight, otherwise it might bolt. Read about bolting on pages 38-39.

Sorrel has a lemony taste.

You can grow herbs, such as rocket and sorrel, as salad vegetables. Or, you could grow Asian leaves, such as mizuna or mustard leaf, as salad.

When the leaves are full and firm, like this, they're ready to pick.

Only cut off the outer leaves of a plant, as new leaves grow from the middle.

Red 'crisphead' cos lettuce

Lollo rossa lettuce

TUMBLING TOMATOES

Some types of cherry tomatoes grow best hanging down over the sides of a container. Here you can find out how to grow them in a hanging basket. They would also grow well in a window box or a tall plant pot – read the instructions opposite.

START:
EARLY SUMMER

SITE:
OUTSIDE SUNNY

FRUITS:
3 MONTHS AFTER PLANTING

YOU WILL NEED:

★ a hanging basket (with a liner) and somewhere sunny to hang it – if you don't have anywhere to hang a basket, use a tall plant pot or a window box – see 'Other containers' opposite

★ a big plant pot or a bucket

★ a 15cm (6in) square of plastic, cut from an old plastic bag

★ multi-purpose compost

★ 1 tumbling cherry tomato plant such as Tumbling Tom, Hundreds and Thousands or Tumbler

★ a small plastic plant pot

★ liquid tomato food

1 Balance the hanging basket on top of the big plant pot or bucket. Put the liner inside and lay the plastic square in the middle. Fill with compost.

2 Make a hole in the middle of the compost and plant the tomato plant (see page 10 for planting tips). Then, push the small plant pot into the compost at the side. Hang in a sunny place outside.

Fill the small plant pot with water. It will soak into the compost.

3 Water the compost really well. After that, water the hanging basket every day. Once a week, add tomato food to the water, following the directions on the packaging.

POTENTIAL PESTS

Lots of different pests like tomato plants. Pick off any you see. For tips to get rid of aphids, see page 15. You can also grow 'companion plants' nearby (see pages 52-53).

----- Aphids

OTHER CONTAINERS

You can grow tumbling tomatoes in a tall plant pot standing on the ground. Use a pot at least 50cm (20in) tall, fill it with multi-purpose compost and follow steps 2-3 opposite.

Or, use a planter that's 20cm (8in) wide and at least as tall, placed on a sunny outside windowsill or a low wall. Fill it with multi-purpose compost and follow steps 2-3.

Hang the basket in a warm, sunny place outside.

As the plant grows, it will hang over the sides of the basket. Flowers will appear.

Tomatoes grow from the flowers. They are green at first.

Most tumbling tomatoes go red when they're ready to eat.

Some tomatoes are ripe when they're orange or yellow. The plant label will tell you.

GROWING HERBS

A herb is a type of plant with a strong, tangy smell and taste. There are lots of different varieties. Some can be grown from seeds; others from pieces of stem cut from bigger plants.

HELPFUL HERBS

Pests such as slugs and snails don't like the strong smell of many herbs. If another plant is being attacked by pests, putting a pot of chives next to it might make the pests go away (see 'Companion plants' on pages 52-53).

Rub a mint or chive leaf between your fingers. Mint leaves have a strong minty smell. Chives smell like a cross between onion and garlic.

If you cut a stem from a mint plant, it can grow into a whole new plant — see opposite.

In the summer, herbs will grow flowers. Bees love to visit herb flowers.

MINT

CHIVES

If your mint plant is growing tall and straggly, cut the tips off long stems. This makes more leaves grow closer to the base.

Chives grow well from seed. If you snip off 3 or 4 spiky leaves at a time, more will grow in their place.

MINT FROM CUTTINGS

YOU WILL NEED:

★ 1 mint plant

★ a small jar

★ a small plant pot at least 10cm (4in) wide, filled with multi-purpose compost. If growing inside, you'll need a drip tray, too.

★ a pencil

TAKE CUTTING:
MARCH-JULY

HARVEST:
JULY-OCTOBER

SITE:
A SUNNY PLACE INSIDE, OR OUTSIDE

1 Cut a healthy-looking, leafy stem from the mint plant. Pull off leaves at the bottom so you have some bare stem.

2 Half-fill your jar with water and put in the mint cutting. Place the jar on a sunny windowsill and wait for the mint to grow roots.

3 When the roots are long and thick, make a hole in the compost with the pencil. Put the mint in the hole, then push compost around it to hold it in place.

CHIVES FROM SEED

YOU WILL NEED:

★ a packet of chive seeds

★ a plant pot at least 10cm (4in) wide filled with multi-purpose compost. If growing inside, you'll need a drip tray, too.

SOW:
MARCH-JUNE

HARVEST:
JUNE-OCTOBER

SITE:
A SUNNY PLACE INSIDE, OR OUTSIDE

1 Water your plant pot. Sprinkle chive seeds in the pot, then cover them with a thin layer of compost.

2 Put the pot in a sunny place. Check the compost every day and water if it feels dry.

USING HERBS

Herbs are used in cooking to add a particular taste to different foods.

For recipes that use chives and mint, go to the Usborne Quicklinks website, www.usborne-quicklinks.com

AIR PLANTS

Air plants are unlike most other plants, as they don't grow in soil. They collect everything they need through their leaves, from air and water. Plants that live in this way are known as 'epiphytes'. Air plants are easy to grow at home – just follow the instructions here.

GROW: SITE:
ANYTIME   INSIDE, LIGHT AND AIRY BUT NOT IN DIRECT SUNLIGHT

1 Choose a jar for your air plant. The plant should have plenty of room. Put the jar in a light, airy place such as a windowsill that's not in direct sunlight for the whole day. Avoid areas near heaters.

2
Your air plant will need watering around once a week (see 'Watering tips'). Fill a bowl with water. Put the air plant in the water with its leaves facing down and its base facing up. Leave for 1 hour.

3
Take the air plant out of the water and stand it in an airy place on a dry towel for 4 hours, until all the water has dried off. Then, put it back in its jar.

WATERING TIPS

If it is hot and dry, your air plant may need watering two or three times a week.

Before you put it back in its jar, make make sure the plant is thoroughly dry, or it may rot.

If you can, use rainwater instead of tap water – put a bowl or small bucket outside to collect it.

You could use a dry facecloth instead of a towel.

You could tie string around the mouth of a jar and hang it up near a window, like this.

There are many different varieties of air plants. You can buy them at some garden centres, or order them online.

In the wild, air plants grow attached to other plants, such as trees. They have small roots that they only use to cling onto the trees.

Your air plant might grow flowers — very small, or slightly bigger, depending on the type of air plant.

One to two months after flowering, an air plant may grow new baby plants, known as 'pups', near the base of the mother plant.

When a pup is half the size of the mother plant, gently twist it to remove it, then put it in its own jar.

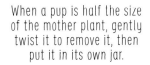

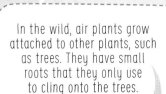

'IN-THE-BAG' POTATOES

Potato plants grow potatoes from their roots underground. They're easy to grow in a bag of compost. For the speediest crop, look for varieties labelled 'First Earlies' and 'Second Earlies', such as Rocket, Red Duke of York, Charlotte, or Anya.

CHITTING (SEE BELOW):
FEBRUARY–MARCH

PLANT:
MARCH–APRIL

HARVEST:
JULY–AUGUST

SITE:
INSIDE THEN
OUTSIDE, SUNNY

YOU WILL NEED:

★ 1 potato for planting, called a 'seed potato'

★ a 20 litre (40lb) bag of multi-purpose compost. If you use a bigger bag, you can grow 2 or 3 potato plants inside it, but ask an adult to help you lift it.

Stand your potato in a cardboard tube.

Shoot

This is known as chitting.

Plant the potato with the shoot pointing up.

Keep the extra compost as you'll need it later.

Cover up the stem until just the tip is showing each time. This is called 'earthing up' (see opposite).

3

1
Your potato plant will be much stronger if the seed potato grows shoots before planting. To do this, leave it in a sunny place.

2
Empty out two-thirds of the compost bag and roll down the sides. Put in the seed potato, cover it with compost, then water well.

Check the compost every 2-3 days to see if it needs watering. As the stem grows, cover it up with compost. Gradually unroll the sides of the bag, too.

4
When the leaves turn brown and the stem starts to droop, this means that your potatoes are fully grown. Tip over the bag and feel around in the compost for them.

Long stems and lots of green leaves mean that your potato is healthy.

Some potato plants grow flowers. This is a sign that the plant is growing lots of potatoes underground.

The stems and leaves of potatoes are poisonous, so don't ever try to eat them.

As the plant grows, potatoes will be growing in the compost bag.

SEED POTATOES

It's best to buy seed potatoes from a garden centre or online. You could grow potatoes you buy in the supermarket for eating, but they might have been sprayed with chemicals to stop them from growing.

EARTHING UP

If growing potatoes get too much sunlight, they turn green and are poisonous. Adding extra compost around the stem, known as 'earthing up', creates a barrier to block out some of the sunlight.

BEE-FRIENDLY FLOWERS

Bees are extremely important for gardeners because they take a powder called pollen from flower to flower. This is called pollination, and it makes plants grow new fruits, vegetables and seeds. Growing flowers that bees like will help all your plants to grow better.

SOW/PLANT:
MARCH–MAY

FLOWER:
JUNE–SEPTEMBER

SITE:
OUTSIDE SUNNY

YOU WILL NEED:

★ a large planter at least 40cm (15in) wide filled with multi-purpose compost

★ 2 bee-friendly plants – see 'Which flowers?' (below) or the plants on these pages for ideas

★ a packet of wildflower seed mix, or 'bee-friendly' seed varieties – see 'Which flowers?' (below) or the plants on these pages for ideas

Bees visit flowers to drink the nectar inside (see below). They get covered in pollen at the same time.

Pollen

Cornflower

As they fly, bees spread pollen from flower to flower. Eventually, this will make more flowers grow.

WHICH FLOWERS?

Bees feed on a sweet liquid called nectar that's produced inside flowers. They like to visit flowers with lots of nectar that's easy to reach.

All the flowers on this page are bee-friendly or wildflower varieties. You could also ask your local garden centre or check online to see which varieties grow well in your area.

Lavender

The plants will grow flowers to give the bees food while the seeds are still growing.

1 Plant your two bee-friendly plants into the compost, making sure there's plenty of space between them.

2 Sow the wildflower or bee-friendly seed varieties over the compost (see page 9 for how to sow small seeds), leaving some space around the plants.

3 In 2-3 weeks you should see shoots from your seeds starting to grow.

Check the compost every 2-3 days and water if it feels dry.

Watch to see how many different bees, and other insects, visit the flowers.

California poppy

Bees love to visit echinacea. But, it's best to grow from a plant rather than seed because it will only flower after it's a year old.

Marjoram

In 2-3 months, the big plants will have flowers.

Continue to water the planter regularly

Gradually, the plants grown from seed will flower, too.

Nigella   Lance leaf coreopsis

ASIAN GREENS

There are lots of leafy green vegetables from China, Japan, India and other Asian countries. They grow quickly, and don't need warm weather. Most work better when it's slightly cool and wet – otherwise, they're likely to bolt (see below).

SOW:
APRIL-JULY OR
AUGUST-SEPTEMBER

HARVEST:
JUNE-OCTOBER OR
SEPTEMBER-NOVEMBER

SITE:
OUTSIDE, IN AN AREA
THAT'S IN SHADE DURING
THE AFTERNOON

YOU WILL NEED:

★ a planter at least 30cm (12in) wide filled with multi-purpose compost

★ a packet of Asian or oriental vegetable seeds – see the opposite page for ideas

Leave the compost in the planter outside overnight before sowing the seeds.

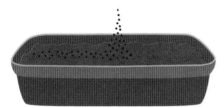

1 Sow the seeds by sprinkling them evenly, then covering them with a thin layer of compost. Make sure the compost is cool.

2 Put the planter in a cool area – somewhere that's in shade during the afternoon is best. Check the compost every other day and water if it feels dry.

3 As the plants grow, cut away the weaker ones until the ones left behind are at least 10cm (4in) apart. Keep watering every other day – don't let the compost dry out.

BOLTING

When plants bolt, they grow long stems and start to produce flowers and seeds, rather than leaves. It happens when they get too hot suddenly, or too dry.
 Traditionally, the plants on these pages grow best in the rainy season of Asian countries, where the climate is mild and damp.

POTENTIAL PESTS

Slugs, snails, caterpillars and flea beetles love to eat Asian greens. See pages 14-15 for how to stop these pests from attacking your plants.

Pak choi grows into a bunch of crisp, green leaves with a crunchy stem. Pick the leaves like 'cut-and-come-again' salad (see pages 26-27), or leave the plant to grow bigger. Then, pick the whole thing.

Garlic chives, also known as Chinese leeks, have a strong garlic taste. If flowers form, snip them off, and the plant will keep growing as normal.

Some plants can bolt and still grow well. Kai lan, or Chinese broccoli, has thick stems and big leaves. When it bolts, it grows tiny flower buds that you can cut off and use in cooking.

Giant red mustard leaves grow well in cool weather over the autumn and winter.

Make sure you keep the plants in an area that's in shade for part of the day, and give them lots of water. Growing them in the cooler months of the year will help, too.

You could look online or in your local garden centre for different varieties of Asian vegetable seeds.

GROWING GERANIUMS

Most people call these plants 'geraniums', though their proper name is 'pelargonium'. They have colourful flowers and are easy to grow from pieces of stem, called cuttings. Don't confuse them with the plants known as 'hardy geraniums', which have softer stems and smaller flowers.

TAKE CUTTINGS:
AUGUST OR SEPTEMBER

FLOWERS:
JUNE- AUGUST

SITE:
INSIDE THEN OUTSIDE, SUNNY

YOU WILL NEED:

★ 1 pelargonium plant (sometimes these are labelled 'geraniums' so check with the seller if you're unsure)

★ a large plant pot around 18cm (7in) wide, filled with multi-purpose compost, plus a drip tray

★ a pencil

★ later, you will also need three medium plant pots, each around 10cm (4in) across, filled with multi-purpose compost

1 Choose a stem that has leaves but no flowers. Cut it off so it's a little longer than your finger. Leave the top two or three leaves and pull off the rest. Do this four more times, so you have five cuttings.

Before

After

2 Take the large pot. Make a hole in the compost with your finger or a pencil. Push in a cutting. Plant the other cuttings too, in a ring. Water so the compost is just moist.

POTENTIAL PESTS

Protect young plants from slugs and snails when you put them outside (see page 14 for tips). When the plants grow, the slugs and snails will leave them alone.

3 Put in a sunny place inside. Water around once a week, so the compost is just moist. Keep on until spring, when new leaves will have grown.

4 Tip out the big pot. Pull the compost apart gently between the plants, leaving some soil around the roots. Plant the three strongest plants in the medium pots. Put outside in a sunny place. Water well.

During the summer, your plants should produce shoots with buds on the ends. These will open into flowers.

When the flowers die, cut them off. This will encourage new flowers to grow.

The flowers will be the same colour as the plant you took your cuttings from.

Water your plants around once a week, so the compost is just moist. Water more often if the weather is hot.

At the end of the summer, you could take more cuttings. Grow them inside over winter, to make more plants for next year.

MINI POND

Plants that only grow in water are known as aquatic plants. Some need just their roots underwater, others have their stems and leaves underwater, too. This project shows you how to make a mini pond where you can grow different types of aquatic plants.

PLANT:
MARCH-JULY

SITE:
SUNNY OUTSIDE

Plants will grow best in rainwater, so you could leave your container outside to fill up when it rains, or use water from a water butt.

FLOATING-LEAVED PLANTS

These grow from the bottom of the pond, with their leaves and flowers resting on the surface of the water. Water crowfoot and fringed water lily are good floating-leaved varieties.

Some aquatic plants can be harmful to wildlife and other plants. Your local garden centre can help you choose the best plants.

SUBMERGED PLANTS

These plants rest on the bottom and only grow a little above the surface. Hornwort or water violet (also known as featherfoil) are good varieties.

Make sure the top stone is above the surface of the water. This allows any animals that may fall into the pond to climb out.

1

Place your container outside. Put a thick layer of gravel in the container, then one of the large stones. Pile the others up on top of each other at one edge. Then, fill the container with tap water, or rainwater.

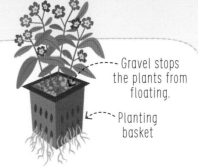

Gravel stops the plants from floating.

Planting basket

2

Add gravel to the tops of the planting baskets. Carefully lower the emergent plant (see below) into the water, on top of one of the large stones.

3
Lower the submerged and floating-leaved plants (see opposite) onto the bottom of the pond.

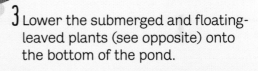

Emergent plant

Submerged plant

Floating-leaved plant

EMERGENT PLANTS

These plants sit in shallow water, then grow with their flowers and leaves above the surface. Grow brooklime, creeping Jenny (also known as moneywort) or water mint plants.

Ponds will attract all kinds of animals — damselflies, dragonflies, water beetles, frogs, newts and more. You could make a list of which animals visit your pond each day.

43

LITTLE PUMPKINS

Pumpkins grow on big, sprawling plants called vines. They need lots of water and food to make them grow well, so small pumpkin varieties are easier for beginners.

Here you can find out how to grow small pumpkins in an ordinary growbag.

SOW:
MAY

HARVEST:
OCTOBER

SITE:
OUTSIDE SUNNY

YOU WILL NEED:

★ 6 seeds from a small pumpkin variety such as Baby Bear, Jack Be Little, Wee B Little or Windsor

★ a growbag

★ a sharp pencil

★ scissors

★ 2 plant pots at least 10cm (4in) wide

1 Use the pencil to poke around 10 big holes in the bottom of the growbag. These are for drainange. Then, turn the bag over.

2 Use scissors to cut a long slit along the middle of the growbag. Plant 3 seeds close together around 2cm (1in) deep at one end. Do the same at the other end. Water well.

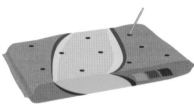

Plant each seed on its side, like this.

POTENTIAL PROBLEMS

Protect your pumpkins from slugs and snails (see page 14 for tips). If you see white, powdery patches on your plants, this may be a fungus called powdery mildew. Water your plants regularly to help avoid it.

3 Check the compost every other day and water it if it feels dry. After around 2 weeks, seedlings will appear. When they are 5cm (2in) high, choose the strongest one at each end of the bag. Pull out the other seedlings and discard them.

4 Press the plant pots into the compost 5cm (2in) away from each seedling. Check the compost every day and if it feels dry, pour water into both the pots. It will soak into the compost gradually.

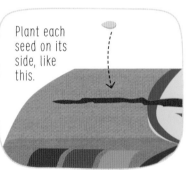

After 6-8 weeks, flowers will appear. They need bees or other insects to visit them, to make pumpkins grow (see pages 36-37).

Make sure there is room around the growbag as the vines will spread beyond the edges.

After the flowers wilt, pumpkins start to grow in their place. They are small and green at first.

As the pumpkins grow, feed them every 10-14 days with liquid plant food that's suitable for vegetables. Mix it with water and pour it into the pots. See page 13 to find out more.

The pumpkins are ready when they are firm and bright orange, and have a hollow sound when you tap them. Cut them off the vine carefully.

If the pumpkins rest on bare earth or grass, put a tile or a piece of wood or plastic underneath them, to prevent them from rotting.

LAYERED BULBS

Here you can find out how to plant different types of bulbs together in one pot. They will flower one after the other, providing a display that lasts from spring to summer.

PLANT:
AUTUMN

FLOWERS:
FEBRUARY TO MAY/JUNE

SITE:
OUTSIDE, SHELTERED THEN SUNNY

YOU WILL NEED:

★ 5 daffodil or narcissus bulbs, preferably an early-flowering variety such as February Gold or Rijnveld's Early Sensation

★ 5 tulip bulbs, preferably a mid-season flowering variety such as Rosy Delight, Prinses Irene or Jan Reus

★ 3 allium bulbs – a variety such as Purple Sensation would work well

★ a frost-proof planter around 30cm (12in) wide and at least as deep

★ multi-purpose compost

★ gardening gloves

1 Put a 10cm (4in) layer of compost in the planter. Arrange the allium bulbs in a single layer, with their pointed ends up. They shouldn't touch each other or the sides of the container. Add an 8cm (3in) layer of compost on

Wear gloves, as bulbs can irritate your skin.

2 Arrange the tulip bulbs on top in the same way. Add a 5cm (2in) layer of compost, then arrange the daffodil bulbs on top in the same way. Add a 5cm (2in) layer of compost on top.

POTENTIAL PESTS

Your bulbs and plants might be attacked by slugs. See page 14 for tips on keeping slugs away.

3 Put outside in a sheltered position, such as next to a wall. Water well. Check every few weeks during the autumn and winter to see if the compost is dry. If it is, water it well.

4 In the early spring, move the planter to a sunny place. Check it every week and water it if the compost feels dry.

The daffodils should flower first, followed by the tulips, and then the alliums last.

Alliums have flowers shaped like pom-poms. They are usually purple or white and smell of garlic.

Tulips have cup-shaped flowers. The colour will depend on the variety of bulb you chose.

Each stem has a bud at the end. It will open out into a flower.

Daffodils have yellow, trumpet-shaped flowers. Some varieties have a delicate scent.

As the bulbs grow, you will see pointed green shoots appear. They will grow into tall stems with long, thin leaves.

OTHER VARIETIES

Don't worry if you can't get early-flowering daffodils and mid-season flowering tulips. It will just mean that some of your tulips, daffodils or alliums might flower at the same time, rather than one after the other.

The shoots of the lower bulbs grow around the bulbs that are higher up.

When the last flowers shrivel, wait for 6 weeks, then cut back the dead leaves and stems. This helps the bulb to store up food for next year.

47

SWEET CORN BLOCK

Sweet corn plants grow vegetables, called corn cobs, that are covered in golden seeds, or kernels. Their pollen is carried by the wind rather than bees, so planting them in a block means that pollen can blow easily from plant to plant.

SOW INSIDE: APRIL-MAY

PLANT OUTSIDE: JUNE

HARVEST: AUGUST-SEPTEMBER

FINAL SITE: OUTSIDE SUNNY

YOU WILL NEED:

★ 8 sweet corn seeds ('supersweet' varieties)

★ 4 small plant pots around 7cm (2½in) wide filled with multi-purpose compost, then placed on drip trays

★ later, a planter at least 50cm (19in) wide and 30cm (12in) deep, filled with multi-purpose compost

1 Water the compost in the four small pots. Push two sweet corn seeds into each pot, then put them on a sunny windowsill. Check the pots every other day and water if the compost feels dry.

In warm weather, sweet corn might need watering every day.

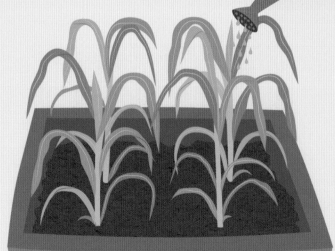

Putting the plants outside gets them used to the slightly cooler weather.

2 When the plants are roughly 4cm (2in) tall, cut away or pull out the weaker one from each pot. Then, remove the drip trays and place the pots outside for a week.

3 Plant the four sweet corns into the planter, at least 22cm (8½in) apart. Check the compost every other day and water if it feels dry.

Flowers, called tassels, grow
at the tops of the sweet corn
plants. The tassels make pollen
(see page 36).

Pollen from the tassels is
blown down onto threads
below, called silks. This makes
corn cobs grow. Silks get
pollen from same plant, and
surrounding ones, too.

Protect young
sweet corns from
slugs and snails.

You could help the pollen from
the tassels drop by shaking the
sweet corn plant, very gently.

A cob grows surrounded by papery
leaves. The kernels are ready in
roughly 2 months, when the silks
turn dark brown.

When you peel away
the leaves, you'll
see golden kernels
covering the cobs.

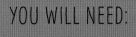

STRAWBERRY STACK

Bunches of strawberries grow on long stalks from bushy plants. This stack allows the fruits to hang down over the sides of the plant pots so they get plenty of sun to ripen.

It's also a good way to grow lots of plants without taking up much space.

PLANT:
MARCH-JUNE

HARVEST:
JUNE-AUGUST

SITE:
OUTSIDE SUNNY

YOU WILL NEED:

★ 8 strawberry plants

★ 1 large plant pot at least 40cm (15in) wide and 30cm (12in) tall

★ 1 medium plant pot, maximum 25cm (10in) wide and 20cm (8in) tall

★ multi-purpose compost

1 Fill the large plant pot three-quarters full of compost. Put the medium pot on top and add compost around it. Then, fill up the medium pot with compost, too.

2 Scoop eight holes out of the compost – five in the bottom pot and three in the top. Then plant strawberry plants in the holes. Give the plants lots of water.

3

As the plants grow, check the compost every two days and water if it's dry. Strawberries are ready to pick when they turn bright red.

POTENTIAL PESTS

Slugs and snails find strawberries as tasty as we do. Putting grit or eggshell around each plant helps keep them off. Pick off any slugs and snails you find on the strawberry plants, or nearby, too (see page 14).

Strawberries grow from the middles of the flowers.

Make sure the stack is in a warm, sunny place.

Bees will help the strawberries to grow. See how you can encourage them to visit your garden on pages 36-37.

RUNNERS

Your strawberry plants may grow shoots, called runners. Plant one or two runners from each plant in a new pot, and they'll grow into a whole new strawberry plant.

Cut them away from the bigger plant one to two weeks after planting.

Strawberries start off small and green. They grow larger, then turn to bright red as they ripen in the sun.

COMPANION PLANTS

Some plants can help to keep other plants healthy, if they are growing close by. They're called 'companion plants'. They help either by keeping away pests, or by attracting gardener-friendly, pest-eating bugs. See below for plants that help other plants in this book.

Dill attracts gardener-friendly bugs including hover flies, ladybirds and pest-eating wasps. Grow it near any herb or vegetable.

Nasturtiums (pages 22-23) can keep aphids away from bean plants (pages 54-55), and whiteflies away from tomatoes (pages 28-29).

Chives (pages 30-31) can help to keep aphids away from sunflowers and tomatoes. They may also deter slugs and snails.

Mint (pages 30-31) is a good companion for tomatoes (pages 28-29), as it can discourage whiteflies and aphids.

FRENCH MARIGOLDS

YOU WILL NEED:

★ a packet of French marigold seeds (Tagetes varieties)

★ 3 plant pots, each at least 15cm (6in) wide, filled with multi-purpose compost

SOW:
APRIL- MAY

SITE:
OUTSIDE SUNNY

FLOWER:
AROUND 10 WEEKS AFTER SOWING

1 Drop 10 seeds onto the compost in each pot. Sprinkle over a little more compost, to cover them. Water well. Put the pot in a sunny place.

2 Check the compost every few days and water it if it feels dry. In two weeks, you should see tiny green seedlings. Leave the biggest four and pull out the rest. Keep watering regularly.

Grow marigolds next to any salad or vegetable. Their smell helps to repel aphids and whiteflies and attracts helpful bugs, too.

COMPANION HERBS

YOU WILL NEED:

★ a packet of dill or chervil seeds

★ 2 plant pots, each at least 10cm (4in) wide, filled with multi-purpose compost

SOW:
APRIL-JUNE

SITE:
OUTSIDE SUNNY

FLOWER:
AROUND 10 WEEKS AFTER SOWING

1 Drop 15-20 seeds onto the compost in each pot. Sprinkle over a little more compost, to cover them. Water well. Put in a sunny place.

2 Check the compost every few days and water it if it feels dry. In two weeks, you should see tiny green seedlings. Keep on watering regularly.

Chervil is good companion plant for tomatoes (pages 28-29) and sunflowers (pages 18-19). The smell can keep aphids away.

CLIMBING BEANS

Climbing bean plants will produce crunchy bean pods in the summer. They have tall, delicate stems that need support. Make a cane wigwam, and watch the stems wind around the canes as they grow.

SOW:
MAY–JUNE

HARVEST:
AUGUST–SEPTEMBER

SITE:
SUNNY OUTSIDE

YOU WILL NEED:

★ a large planter at least 40cm (16in) tall and 30cm (11in) wide filled with multi-purpose compost

★ 8 seeds from a French climbing bean variety, such as Sultana, Blue Lake or Blauhide

★ 4 bamboo canes, at least 2m (6½ft) tall

★ elastic band

★ string

1

To make your cane wigwam, wrap an elastic band around the canes. Spread out the cane ends and push them down into the planter.

Wrap around the elastic band towards the tops of the canes.

2

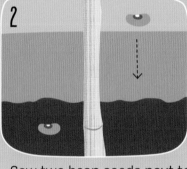

Sow two bean seeds next to each cane by pushing them down into the compost. Water well.

3

As the plants grow, cut away the weaker plant next to each cane. Then, use string to tie the remaining stems onto the canes.

POTENTIAL PESTS

Slugs and snails love to eat young bean shoots. Bean plants are also attacked by aphids. Turn to pages 14–15 to find out how to protect your beans from pests.

Check for aphids under the bean leaves and on the stems.

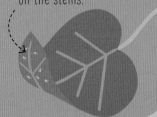

When the bean stems reach the tops of the canes, cut them off. This is called 'pinching out'. It makes the plant use its energy to grow more flowers and beans, rather than a very tall stem.

Adding cane toppers on the tops of the canes will stop people poking or hurting themselves (see page 7).

As the petals of the flowers droop and fall off, tiny beans will start to form in the middle.

Pick the beans when they're around 10cm (4in) long, and they feel firm. Picking the beans regularly will make lots more beans grow.

You can help plants cling to the canes by gently winding the stems around them.

Bean plants love lots of water – check the compost every 3-4 days. Once beans start to grow, they need more water, so check every day.

55

SUCCULENTS

Succulents are plants with thick, fleshy leaves, stems or roots. They often grow happily in very dry conditions, either inside or outside.

Here you'll find out how to grow small succulent plants in a pot.

PLANT:
SPRING OR SUMMER

SITE:
INSIDE OR OUT, SUNNY

FLOWERS:
OCCASIONALLY, IN SUMMER

YOU WILL NEED:

★ two or three small succulent plants such as sempervivums (best if you live in a place with cold winters) or echeverias (best if you live in a place with mild winters)

★ a plant pot at least 15cm (6in) wide

★ if you're growing your succulents inside, you'll need a drip tray

★ multi-purpose compost

★ fine gravel or horticultural grit

1 Half-fill your pot with compost. Add gravel or grit so the pot is three-quarters full. Mix the gravel or grit and the compost together.

2 Scoop out three holes in the compost, spaced well apart. Plant your succulent plants (see page 10 for planting tips). Sprinkle a ½cm (¼in) deep layer of gravel or grit over the surface of the compost.

3 Water the pot. Once a week, feel the compost. If it feels completely dry, water it. If it feels moist, leave it.

When you feel the compost, push your finger down past the gravel layer.

WHY SUCCULENT?

Succulent means something that's thick and juicy – like the leaves of succulent plants. The moisture is locked inside a tough coating, which helps the plants stay moist even in dry conditions.

This picture shows a succulent leaf sliced in half.

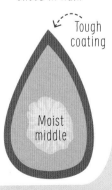

Tough coating

Moist middle

Keep the pot in a warm, sunny place.

After 3 years, some types of succulents may flower in the summer.

Succulents come in many colours and varieties. You could choose three different ones

BABY SUCCULENTS

Baby plants may grow on long, trailing stems, or next to the original plants. When they measure 2.5cm (1in) across, gently pull them off. Then, plant them in a new pot of their own.

If you keep the pot inside, stand it in a drip tray.

GARLIC BULBS

Garlic is a plant that grows a round bulb underground, made up of lots of sections, called cloves. People use garlic cloves in cooking. Garlic plants have long, green stems and leaves that have a strong, garlicky smell. Some varieties will grow round, spiky flowers, too.

SOW:
OCTOBER-EARLY DECEMBER

HARVEST:
LATE JUNE-JULY

SITE:
OUTSIDE SUNNY

YOU WILL NEED:

★ 1 garlic bulb for planting, of either a softneck or hardneck variety (see 'Hard or soft?' opposite)

★ a large planter at least 40cm (15in) wide and 40cm (15in) deep

★ multi-purpose compost

★ fine gravel or horticultural grit

1 Fill your planter a quarter full with gravel. Add compost on top to fill it. Then, mix it all together.

2 Break off 4 cloves from the bulb of garlic. Separate them out, being careful not to peel off the papery skin.

Make sure the rounded end is pointing down and the cloves are spaced well apart.

3 Push the garlic cloves into the compost until their tops are just below the surface. Put in a sunny place, then water.

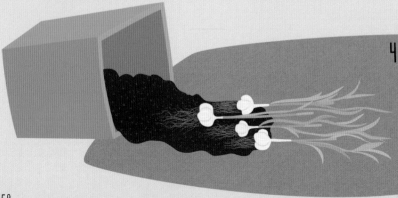

4 The plants will grow tall stems. Some varieties will grow flowers, too (see opposite). The bulbs are fully grown when the leaves droop and turn yellow. Tip over the container to get to the bulbs.

This is what a hardneck scape (see below) looks like. If you want your garlic bulbs to grow bigger, cut off the scapes (it won't damage the plant). The scapes have a mild, garlicky taste and can be used in cooking.

You could leave the scapes (see below) on the plant to turn into spiky, ball-shaped flowers. Bees and butterflies love to visit them.

Softnecks should just grow leaves. If you see any flowers forming, this means that the plant is starting to die. Cutting off the flower might save it.

Lots of garden pests don't like the smell or taste of garlic. Putting garlic next to plants pests like to eat may help to protect the plants.

Garlic bulbs will rot if they get too wet. The gravel will help water drain away, but make sure you only water when the compost feels dry.

HARD OR SOFT?

There are two varieties of garlic – softneck and hardneck. Softneck garlics don't usually grow flowers. But hardnecks grow flower shoots, called scapes.

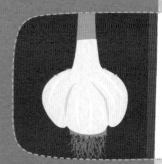

In the compost, each clove will grow into a new bulb made up of lots of cloves.

COMPOST AND PLANT FOOD

You can grow all the plants in this book using bought compost and plant food. But you could also make your own using garden and household leftovers.

COMPOST

Compost is made from the broken-down remains of old plants, paper and cardboard. You will need a mixture of 'greens' and 'browns' – see below. Don't add cooked food, meat, fish, cheese, bones, weeds, diseased plants, bulbs, hard stems or wood.

Put your compost bin or heap in a place that is in shade in the summer.

It's easiest to stack your greens and browns into a heap. But if you have a compost bin with an open base, use that instead, following the instructions below.

Always use bought compost when you are sowing seeds.

GREENS

Vegetable peelings

Fruit trimmings or peelings

Grass cuttings

Trimmings from garden plants – but only small, soft pieces

BROWNS

Dry autumn leaves

Straw

Newspaper and cardboard, torn into small pieces

Make a layer of browns, then a thinner layer of greens, and so on.

Cover the top with sheets of thick cardboard, such as flattened cardboard boxes. This will keep it warm and help it to break down more quickly.

Compost heap

Browns

Greens

Wet each layer well as you make it.

Once a month, use a garden spade or fork to mix and turn everything. Scrape everything back into a heap. Add more water if it looks dry, then cover with cardboard again.

Eventually everything will break down into crumbly, dark compost that smells like fresh soil. This may take from 6 months to a year.

PLANT FOOD

You can make your own plant food by leaving garden weeds in water. The goodness from the weeds seeps into the water. You will need a plant pot and a bucket with a tightly-fitting lid.

Collect some weed leaves. Put them in a plastic plant pot or other plastic container with drainage holes.

Put the container inside the bucket. Add water, so the leaves are completely covered. Put on the lid.

After 6 weeks, open the lid. Lift up the container, so all the smelly liquid drains back into the bucket. Add the slimy dead weeds to your compost heap.

Hold your nose! The mixture will be VERY SMELLY.

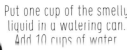

Put one cup of the smelly liquid in a watering can. Add 10 cups of water.

Then, water it onto your plants.

LEAF MOULD

You can make a simple compost known as leaf mould, using dead autumn leaves. It's easier to make than normal compost, but it can take a lot longer.

Collect lots of dead autumn leaves. Wait until they are wet from rain, or wet them with a watering can.

Put them in a big plastic bin bag. Tie up the top. Carefully poke lots of holes in the bag using a garden fork.

Put the bag in a sheltered spot. Leave it for one to two years.

It's ready when the leaves have turned crumbly and dark brown and look like compost.

Leaf mould helps to keep compost moist and plants healthy.

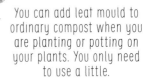

You can add leaf mould to ordinary compost when you are planting or potting on your plants. You only need to use a little.

GLOSSARY

This glossary explains some useful gardening words that are used in the book.

air plant A plant that doesn't need soil, and takes everything it needs from air and water.

aquatic plant A plant that grows with its roots and/or leaves and stem in water.

aphids Small bugs that swarm onto plants and feed on sap (see *sap*). Aphids can stop a plant growing properly.

Asian vegetable A vegetable originally from Asia that grows best in cool, damp conditions.

blackflies Aphids that are black in colour.

bolting When some leafy vegetable plants start to die and grow long stems, flowers and seeds.

bud A young flower, before it's opened.

bulb A tight bundle of leaves from which roots, stems and flowers grow.

chitting Leaving a seed potato to grow shoots before planting it.

clove A section of a garlic bulb that is planted to grow a garlic plant.

companion plant A plant that helps to stop garden pests from attacking other plants.

compost Broken down plant material, cardboard or paper that plants are grown in.

cut-and-come-again A type of lettuce or other leafy vegetable that can grow more leaves when some of its leaves are cut.

cutting A stem or part of a stem that's cut from a plant and used to grow a new plant.

dividing Separating two plants grown in the same pot.

drip tray A dish placed under a plant pot to collect any water that seeps through the compost.

earthing up Covering growing potatoes with compost to stop them getting too much sunlight.

edible flower A flower that you can eat.

flea beetle Tiny beetles that chew holes in the leaves of some plants.

garden pest A bug or animal that eats or attacks plants, weakening them, or killing them completely.

gardener-friendly bug A bug that helps plants to grow, by spreading pollen or by eating pests that attack plants.

greenflies Aphids that are green in colour.

grow bag A compost-filled bag in which plants can be grown.

hanging basket A hanging container used to grow plants with trailing stems.

harvesting Picking leaves, seeds, vegetables or fruits when they're ready to eat or use.

herb A plant with a strong, tangy smell and taste. Herbs are often used in cooking.

horticultural grit/fine gravel Small stones used for lots of different things, including helping water to drain quickly through compost.

leaf scorch When a plant's leaf turns brown and dies after it gets wet, then very hot.

micro-leaf A plant that's picked after its first leaves grow.

mould A disease that can be caused by a plant getting too wet, or its roots sitting in too much water.

nectar A sweet liquid inside a plant. Bees and butterflies feed on it.

plant food Something that's given to plants to help them grow.

pinching out Cutting off the top of a plant to help the leaves and fruit lower down to grow more quickly.

pollen A powder inside flowers. When pollen is spread from one flower to another, it makes the plant grow new seeds, fruits or vegetables.

pollination When pollen is spread from flower to flower, either by bugs or the wind.

potting on Moving a plant from a smaller pot into a bigger one.

powdery mildew A disease that is a white fungus growing on the leaves and stem of a plant.

ripe When a fruit, vegetable or seed on a plant is fully grown and ready to be picked.

root Part of a plant that grows down into the compost and sucks up water and food.

runner A shoot that will grow into a new plant. Only some plants, such as strawberries, grow these.

sap The liquid inside plants. Aphids and some other pests feed on sap.

scape A garlic bud, before it opens into a flower.

seed potato A potato that's planted to grow a new potato plant.

seedling A young plant, usually with only a few leaves and a short stem.

shoot A new stem, either after it's just grown above the surface of the compost, or from an existing stem.

sowing Planting a seed in compost.

succulent A plant with thick, fleshy leaves, stems or roots that grows well in dry conditions.

thinning out Cutting away smaller or weaker plants to make sure only the strongest and healthiest ones continue to grow.

vine A long, trailing stem that some vegetable or fruit plants grow.

whiteflies Small bugs, similar to aphids, that swarm onto a plant and suck out the sap (see *sap*). Whiteflies can stop plants growing properly.

INDEX

Art Director: Mary Cartwright

Every effort has been made to trace the copyright holders of material in this book. If any rights have been omitted, the publishers offer to rectify this in any subsequent editions following notification.